Guard Your Heart

Guard Your Heart

By Kathy Lynette Shorter

Harrison House Publishers
Tulsa, Oklahoma

Guard Your Heart
ISBN 1-57794-051-2
Copyright © 1997 by Kathy Lynette Shorter
P.O. Box 44800
Tacoma, WA 98444

Published by Harrison House, Inc.
P. O. Box 35035
Tulsa, Oklahoma 74153

Acknowledgment

I would like to thank Barbara Anderson for the hours she put into typing the manuscript of this book. And a very special thanks to Dr. Betty R. Price, my example of a godly woman, mother, and pastor's wife, for taking the time to read the manuscript for *Guard Your Heart*, and writing the forward for this book.

Contents

Steps To Receive Jesus as Your Personal Savior

Foreword

Guard Your Heart tells you how to protect your heart from the lust of the flesh, the lust of the eyes, and the pride of life. It reveals how you can be free from a low self-image, an inferiority complex, and depression. Your faith will be strengthened and you will be encouraged to walk in victory as you study this easy-to-read book.

By Dr. Betty Price

Introduction

Most people spend their entire life working hard, long hours to gain material wealth. Yet they spend so little time, if any, working on their spiritual wealth.

There is nothing wrong with working. In fact, the Bible says that if you don't work, you don't eat. (2 Thessalonians 3:10.) It also says that you should provide for your family and leave an inheritance to your children's children. (Proverbs 13:22.)

All of these principles are in the Word of God. But when you put work first — when you put more importance on gaining material wealth and seeking material things than you do on seeking God — then you are headed for trouble and sorrow.

What you can gain with your own hands can never give you peace or the things that mean the most in life, such as a good home, a great marriage, children who love you, and, most importantly, eternal life. But when you put God first and you keep your other priorities in their proper order, you can have the spiritual blessings *and* the material blessings.

In fact, the Bible says that material blessings shall be added unto you: **But seek ye first the kingdom of God, and his righteousness; and all these things shall be added unto you** (Matthew 6:33). God will add the material things you need; He gives the increase in your life.

As you read through this book, you will discover

how important your heart is. When the word *heart* is used in this book, you will know that I am talking about your most important heart — your spiritual heart (your human spirit), and not the physical heart, which will eventually stop.

Your physical heart will one day be of no use to you anymore. It is only useful while you are here on this earth. When you die and can no longer gain material things, what you have acquired in this world will become unusable to you. And someone else may start using what took you many years to accumulate. That is why I believe the Bible asks us the question: **For what shall it profit a man, if he shall gain the whole world, and lose his own soul?** (Mark 8:36).

Therefore, we must prioritize what we care so much about. We can get so caught up with what we can *see* that we forget about the things we cannot see.

If you were to put your hand to your chest where your heart is located, you would feel it pumping. You can't see your heart pumping, but you can surely feel it. (If you can't, and you are reading this, please call me right now. I want to hear about this miracle!)

We often tend to put more value on that which we can see or feel. I would like to submit to you this thought: What you *can't* feel or see is of much value. That is why we are to walk by faith and not by sight. Your faith is very valuable. We limit God when we live by our five senses: taste, touch, sight, hearing and smell.

While we look not at the things which are seen, but at the things which are not seen: for the things which are seen are temporal; but the things which are not seen are eternal.

2 Corinthians 4:18

It is not the physical heart that is the most important, even though you cannot physically live without it.

It is your spiritual heart, or your human spirit. When you accept the Lord into your life, your spirit is born again. You were once doomed to go to hell, but now you will enter into heaven.

Now that your spirit is born again, you have a new citizenship. You are part of royalty. You are now in the kingdom of God. Your marching orders should come straight from the throne room by way of the Spirit of God. And when you listen and obey the Holy Spirit, your negative circumstances will change. Your life will take on a whole new meaning as you discover your purpose for being on this earth.

Just think about it. What if everyone in this world were a part of the kingdom of God and obeyed God's commands? No more jails, locks on the doors, or attorneys would be needed. Divorce courts and child-protective services would be a thing of the past. And I could go on and on.

If only we were all governed by the Word of God. If we were governed by God's Word, we would have no need to be governed by the laws of this land. But, unfortunately, it isn't like this. Many Christians and non-Christians alike choose not to live by the Word of God. Therefore, we are governed by the laws of the land, which really is a lesser law.

Therefore, with all the chaos that is in the world, you must guard your heart. Once again, when I say the word *heart*, I am talking about the real you, the spirit person inside you that cannot be seen. (I will note it otherwise if I am talking about your physical heart.)

You are a three-part person: You live in a body; you possess a soul (which consists of your mind, will, and emotions); but you are a spirit. And as I mentioned earlier, your spirit cannot be seen.

There is one main thing I want you to remember throughout this book: You must learn to guard your heart.

You are living out the things that you have allowed to enter your heart. Either you are living the life of God, which includes faith, peace, joy, love, prosperity and all good gifts (James 1:17), or you are living a defeated life, which only Satan can give and which includes bitterness, poverty, confusion, doubt, hate and anything else that is the opposite of good.

You chose death when you allowed the cares of the world and other things that are against God's Word to settle in your heart. The Bible says that God's people perish because of a lack of knowledge. (Hosea 4:6.) That means that some people just don't know how important their heart is; they don't understand the great need to guard it. Then others have the knowledge, but they reject the truth and allow the cares of this world to rob them of their God-given rights to enjoy life.

I believe the reading of this book is a divine appointment for you. That doesn't mean this book is the most important book you could ever read. The Bible is the most important book in the world to read, study and meditate on; you should make it your lifelong goal to do so, because God's Word *is* your life.

However, I believe this book will accomplish an important purpose: It will cause you to become aware of the importance of guarding your heart. After reading it, you will no longer just pass over scriptures pertaining to the heart of man when you are studying God's Word. Those scriptures will jump at you with a force that will change your life, little by little, as it did mine.

I was a desperate person with a broken heart, and the power of God healed my heart. Instead of seeking a man to go to, I went right to the Source, the One who created man. It was the power of God that totally healed me emotionally and mended my broken heart. I believe

God will do the same for you if you will allow Him to.

Now that I am healed of a broken heart, I realize how important it is to guard my heart all the time, 7 days a week, 24 hours a day, 365 days a year. It is a lifestyle. I will show you why and how to guard your heart, using the Word of God as your foundation. It is a solid foundation that will stand throughout eternity.

He [the person who hears and obeys God's Word] is like a man which built an house, and digged deep, and laid the foundation on a rock: and when the flood arose, the stream beat vehemently upon that house, and could not shake it: for it was founded upon a rock.

Luke 6:48

Your life must be founded on the Rock. That Rock is Jesus, and Jesus is the Word made flesh. God's Word will never fade and will never weaken; it is a sure foundation.

Chapter 1

Issues of Life

Keep thy heart with all diligence; for out of it are the issues of life.

Proverbs 4:23

God commands us in this scripture to do something with our heart. When God commands us to do something in His Word, we just need to do it, because it is for our own good and the good of those who are around us.

We are told to keep our heart with all diligence. What does this mean? It is so important to understand what God means. When He reveals something to us through His Word, it will totally change our lives if we will apply that revelation to our daily lives.

When you enter into a dark room, the first thing you try to find is the light switch. Why? Because it isn't fun walking around in a dark room. You could bump into something, trip over something, or even hurt yourself or someone else. But as soon as you turn on the light switch, you can see what is in the room. You can walk to the place you need to go to without any problem.

That is how it is with the Word of God. When the Holy Spirit reveals a truth to your heart (your spirit), in that area you can now clearly see. And you can apply that truth to avoid an accident or a misstep in your life.

This is so important for you to grab ahold of.

Once Proverbs 4:23 is revealed to you, it will become your foundation to build upon. You will no longer be in darkness in this area of guarding your heart, but in the light.

We are to *keep* our heart. Another meaning for the word *keep* in the Hebrew is "to guard and protect."[1] When we guard and protect our heart, we keep them from getting polluted.

Our hearts are sensitive. The *Webster's Dictionary* meaning of the word *sensitive* is "susceptible to the ideas, emotions, or circumstances of others; capable of perceiving with a sense or senses; easily offended, touchy."

I want you to know how valuable your heart is. Satan knows what will happen when the right things — the truth of God's Word — get into your heart. Your heart is where the Word of God must settle. When God's Word abides in your heart, it becomes very valuable.

When God's truth is revealed to you, as it is this very minute, you must guard and protect your heart at all times so that you will succeed in this world and have life more abundantly.

You see, in the world, you can have a form of life, but in Jesus Christ, you can have the God-kind of life (or the life of God, as the Bible puts it). The world can offer a form of success, but in God you can have *good* success (the God-kind of success as described to Joshua 1:8).

When your heart becomes valuable to you, you won't allow just anything to enter in. You will guard and protect it, allowing only the truth of God's Word to enter in and stay there. Then your heart will become sensitive, but not to the things I just listed from the *Webster Dictionary*: not to the ideas, emotions, or the circumstances of others.

Your heart will become less dependent on your sense knowledge and your five senses. It won't be easily

---

[1]Strong, James. "Hebrew and Chaldee Dictionary." *In Strong's Exhaustive Condordance of the Bible*, Nashville: Thomas Nelson Publishers, 1990, p. 80.

offended or touchy. Instead, your heart will stay sensitive to the Spirit of God, ready and willing to yield to God with every breath you breathe.

That is why I believe our hearts were created to be sensitive, not to the world's pollution, but to the Spirit of God.

Some people have allowed their heart to become hardened because of the cares of the world and sin.

But exhort one another daily, while it is called Today; lest any of you be hardened through the deceitfulness of sin.

Hebrews 3:13

When your heart is hardened because of the deceitfulness of sin, it becomes less sensitive to the voice of God and more sensitive to your five senses. When you can't hear the voice of God, you can't be led. This is not a normal state to be in as a Christian, because Jesus said, "My sheep know My voice." (John 10:14,27.)

We are Jesus' sheep, and we need to be led by the voice of God speaking to our heart. And not only is it extremely important for us to be led by the Spirit of God, but according to Mark 6:52, we can actually lose our understanding of God's Word if we allow our hearts to harden.

Now you can see why it is important to guard your heart and how quickly you can be defeated if you don't. There is nothing wrong with godly sensitivity. It shouldn't take much for God to get your attention. Then once you hear His voice, you must quickly become a doer of the Word. Hearing and obeying should be synonymous terms for a born-again Christian.

God speaks, you hear, and then you obey — no questions asked and with no hesitation. How do you know you are hearing from God? Because when He speaks, He will always back up His spoken Word with

His written Word.

Proverbs 4:23 says that you must guard your heart and protect it, keeping it with all diligence, because out of it will come your lifestyle (or issues of life). Now let's look at the word *issue*. The Hebrew meaning of the word *issue* means "source; going forth; outgoings."[2]

In other words, what is going out of you? Just take a quick inventory of your life and ask yourself the question, "What is going forth from my life?" But you must be honest with yourself. Is strife going forth from your life? How about bitterness, revenge, lack of joy, poor self-image, jealousy, lack of trust, hurt, painful memories of the past, bad relationships, or unforgiveness?

Whatever is going forth from you is what you have allowed to settle in your heart and take root. If wrong things have taken root, they can and will harden your heart, if you allow them to.

You may say to yourself, "I don't have any of those harmful things just mentioned going forth from my life. I have overcome in those areas." If that is true, then I would say to you that you have made a practice of guarding your heart in those areas. But make sure you keep guarding your heart; you can never let it go unattended.

Keep thy heart with all diligence; for out of it are the issues of life.

Proverbs 4:23

You must still keep your heart even after you have gotten the victory. Your spirit (heart) is at war with your flesh. Remember, your spirit is born again (if not, I will give you the opportunity to receive salvation at the end of this book). It is connected to God's Spirit, which is the Holy Spirit. Galatians 5:17 says,

---

[2]Strong, James. "Hebrew and Chaldee Dictionary." *In Strong's Exhaustive Condordance of the Bible*, Nashville: Thomas Nelson Publishers, 1990, p. 123.

> **For the flesh lusteth against the Spirit, and the Spirit against the flesh: and these are contrary the one to the other: so that ye cannot do the things that ye would.**
>
> **Galatians 5:17**

In Galatians 5:19-21, it lists all the works of the flesh — sins that issue forth from our lives when we do not guard our hearts. But if we guard our hearts against the things of the flesh, then the fruit of the Spirit, those issues of life listed in Galatians 5:22, will come forth from our lives.

If you allow negativity to come into your life, then only negativity will come out of it; whatever goes in must come out.

You must watch even the thoughts of your heart. Did you know that your heart thinks?

In Acts 8, starting at verse 14, it tells a story about a sorcerer named Simon. When Simon saw people receiving the Holy Spirit as the apostles laid hands on them, he wanted this power as well. Simon offered the apostles money for this gift. Peter, one of the apostles, replied,

> **...Thy money perish with thee, because thou hast thought that the gift of God may be purchased with money.**
>
> **Acts 8:14**

Then Peter told Simon that his heart was not right in the sight of God. Peter told him to repent of this wickedness and to pray to God, **...if perhaps the thought of thine heart may be forgiven thee** (v. 22).

Whatever is in abundance in your heart will come out. Simon wanted the power the apostles possessed, but for the wrong reasons. And he really couldn't help asking. He had an abundance of greed in his heart, so that greed had to come out.

We can see this principle of "whatever is in abundance in the heart must come out" also acted out in the lives of the Israelites. Let's look at what the Word says about them in Acts 7.

This passage of Scripture talks about the children of Israel when they were delivered from Egypt. The Israelites had been slaves in Egypt for hundreds of years. Then God raised up a leader named Moses to lead Israel out of Egypt. So God's people were led *out of Egypt*, but Egypt was not yet *out of their hearts*.

Whom [God] **our fathers would not obey, but rejected. And IN THEIR HEARTS THEY TURNED BACK TO EGYPT.**

Acts 7:39, NKJV

The children of Israel didn't physically turn back or go back to Egypt. The desire for Egypt was still *in their hearts*.

Egypt represents an unguarded heart; Egypt represents bondage. An unguarded heart will put you into bondage, and sooner or later that "bondage thinking" will come out of you.

Once again I submit this question to you: What is going forth, or what is the outgoing, from your life? Whatever is the abundance in your heart, it will eventually come out: **...for out of the abundance of the heart the mouth speaketh** (Matthew 12:34). Therefore, you must guard and protect your heart from the wrong abundance and allow the right issues of life to accumulate abundantly in your heart.

You will constantly have negative forces coming at you, because you live in a world that is under a curse. But God has already given you everything you need to guard and protect your heart. He has given His Spirit to lead you and to always cause you to triumph in Christ. (2 Corinthians 2:14.) And most importantly, He has given you His Word.

The only way to make sure that good things are accumulating in your heart is to test everything in line with God's Word. That's why knowing your rights as a child of God becomes very important to you. Get to know your rights in the Word of God. A lack of knowledge will only cause you to perish in various areas of life.

Let me share a personal testimony of why it is important to guard your heart and what will happen if you don't guard it. My testimony will reveal that allowing the wrong things to issue forth from your life will destroy you.

This is just a small part of my testimony, but I feel it will bless you. Some of you may relate to my experiences. As you respond to God, you can receive your deliverance, too.

I was born out of wedlock. I didn't find this out until I was eighteen years old. After learning about this fact, for several years thereafter I tried to gather information about my physical birth.

The one story I was told that I can remember was that my biological mother was not married and that she had an affair with a married military man. She was poor; in fact, I was told that she was a maid and couldn't keep me, so she gave me away when I was just an infant.

When this story was told to me, I was shocked. I didn't guard my heart; instead, I allowed hurt, rejection, a poor self-image, hate, and rebellion to enter in. I really felt like a nobody; I felt so ashamed.

I was a Christian at the time, but I had not been taught the Word of God, so I didn't know some very important, simple truths. For instance, I didn't know that God's anointing is here to heal the brokenhearted and that I could go to Him and cast my cares upon Him. I was never taught about this anointing or told that God's anointing will destroy the yoke of the enemy. I can't remember how many yokes were causing me to be defeated at the time, but there were many.

The Bible says that **...faith comes by hearing, and hearing by the word of God** (Romans 10:17, NKJV). How could I have faith for something I had never heard about?

It is so important for pastors to teach the people who God puts in their care that they can have victory in any area of life. Thank God for pastors who are teaching the truth!

I had accepted the Lord at the early age of fourteen. But when I learned about the circumstances of my birth at age eighteen, I was desperate for help; I just didn't know much about the Word. (Of course, this is partially my fault, too, because we are responsible to learn what God is saying to us through His Word).

At the church I went to, everyone just shouted and stayed in church a lot, and the women were told not to wear makeup. That is honestly all I can remember learning about in church. This is not a put-down against that church. I am just sharing my testimony.

So I turned against God, because I thought that He had failed me. I thought all people were just liars. I couldn't trust people, and I had no trust for God.

My unguarded heart started to lead me into an unhealthy body. I tried to drown my sorrow with food, and I started to gain weight quickly. I developed ulcers. I hated life and didn't care about being honest anymore. I hated people because I hated myself, and then I allowed anxieties to rule my life.

Proverbs 12:25 says, **Heaviness** [anxiety] **in the heart of man maketh it stoop** [causes depression]: **but a good word maketh it glad.** All I needed was a good word, a word from God.

Depression almost took my life. I just wanted out, and here I was only eighteen years old. If this is where you are right now, keep reading, because God has a good word for you!

Several months after the news I received about my birth, my fiancee sent for me (I was in another state), and we got married. But my husband couldn't heal my broken heart.

Marriage can't set you free. Neither can drugs or alcohol. No person and no natural thing can set you free. There is only one Freedom-giver, and that is God.

For six months, I stayed in the apartment where we were living in at the time with no television or telephone to entertain me. My husband was working three jobs, so he was not home very often. I had a lot of free time (which I now believe God allowed me to have), and I used it to cry out to God.

I was angry with God. I talked to Him about what upset me, and I talked to Him about the people I hated. On and on I went, pouring my heart out to God for months.

What I was actually doing was casting my care on the Lord. I didn't know the Word of God at the time, but His Spirit was leading me to freedom — and I am telling you, casting your cares on the Lord works!

Casting all your care upon Him; for He careth for you.

1 Peter 5:7

You are not to cast *some* of your care on the Lord, but *all* of it — everything.

I did just that. I told God that I hated myself. I told Him how I wanted to forgive, but needed help to do it. I just talked to God as if He were a close friend whom I could really trust (which He is!).

I can't remember all that I said and asked, because

it has been more than twenty years. But I know that I cast all my cares on the Lord, and, therefore, I felt a release. It wasn't long afterwards that I started to lose the weight I had gained, and I was physically healed of ulcers.

Negative words spoken against me while I was growing up that surfaced in my adult years were destroyed by the power of God. But I had to hear and learn the Word of God to be set free in this area of my life. I also had to learn God's Word so that many other yokes could be destroyed, such as a poor self-image. Again and again over the years, God would lead me to His Word, and He would reveal truth to me. The Bible says this:

...you shall know the truth, the truth shall make you free.

John 8:32, NKJV

For example, when I read John 1:12 and 13, the Spirit of God revealed the truth to me through His Word.

But as many as received Him, to them he gave the right to become children of God, to those who believe in His name:

who were born, not of blood, nor of the will of the flesh, nor of the will of man, but of God.

John 1:12,13, NKJV

Through this scripture, I realized that my spiritual birth was more important than my physical birth. It was God's will that I was born again. I was ashamed of my physical birth. I was born by the will of the flesh, and I may add that it was *a lot* of flesh. Actually, I was a product of sin, and for years I was so ashamed that I would lie about how I was born. I couldn't even utter the words out of my mouth that I was born out of wedlock.

Now look what God has done; I am writing this in a book for the world to read. Praise God, I am no longer ashamed! There are a lot of children who were born into this world the way I was. Those children need to hear that they can be born again, but this time by the will of God. God will give them the right to become *His* children.

It is a blessing for me to know that God is my Father. I don't physically know who my biological parents are. For years I wanted to know, but that is not my desire anymore. If one day I find out, great; but if not, that's okay too.

There is nothing wrong with trying to find out this information. But so many people are so stressed out and full of hurt because they don't know who their biological parents are.

I decided to guard my heart in this area and allow God's Word to have first place.

Because of my own experience, I can honestly tell you that God will meet any need you have. He will fill every void. I have come to know my Heavenly Father, and He is the One whom I want to get to know more and more.

I thank God for my adopted parents, and I have prayed for my birth parents, that they may come to a saving knowledge of Jesus Christ and give their lives to Him (if they are still alive and can do so). But I don't worry about the past (and you shouldn't either); I cast that care on Him years ago.

Remember, *all* of your care is to be cast on the Lord. And when He has your care — you don't! When you cast your care on the Lord, is that denial? No, it is faith in God, and the just shall live by faith. (Romans 1:17.) You are justified because of what Jesus did for you; you received the gift of salvation. Now you must order your life by faith. That is how you guard your heart.

I received another revelation from the Lord that helped me to overcome the past. Yes, I was born out of wedlock and I was a person conceived by the act of adultery, which is sin to God. True, a person habitually living this kind of lifestyle cannot enter into the kingdom of God unless he repents and turns away from his sins. If he will do that, God will forgive him of his sins and cleanse him of all unrighteousness.

The reason I am saying all of this is that the statement I'm about to make might be misunderstood very easily. However, I believe that this scripture will help many of you.

Before I formed thee in the belly I knew thee; and before thou camest forth out of the womb I sanctified thee, and I ordained thee a prophet unto the nations.

Jeremiah 1:5

Now, of course, God was talking to the prophet Jeremiah in this verse. But I believe these words are also for us.

I believe that the act of sin committed before I was born was against God, but that God turned a negative situation around for His glory. I was conceived in sin, but I was called from my mother's womb. I then accepted that call at age fourteen.

Now I am able to use my testimony to help other children and adults who are born out of wedlock to know that God has not left them, and that it wasn't their choice to be born this way. I tell them that they don't have to be ashamed of a sin that they didn't commit. But the most important thing for them to realize is that God wants them to be born again, adopted into His family so they can live eternally and receive a life here on earth filled with blessings and victories.

...I am come that they might have life, and that they might have it more abundantly.

John 10:10

One more scripture I want to give you on this subject is found in Psalm 139.

> **For thou hast possessed my reins: thou hast covered me in my mother's womb.**
>
> **I will praise thee; for I am fearfully and wonderfully made: marvelous are thy works; and that my soul knoweth right well.**
>
> **Psalm 139:13,14**

God took care of you in your mother's womb. He possessed your *reins*, which means that God formed your inward parts. That's why you are to praise Him for His marvelous works.

Take time out right now to thank God for your physical birth, no matter how you were conceived, and then thank Him for your spiritual birth! First, you had to be physically born before you could become spiritually born. Thank God for both types of birth, but you still must be born again (spiritually) to have eternal life.

You must learn the thoughts of God and what He thinks about you. The Bible says that God's thoughts are higher than our thoughts. And not only His thoughts are higher than ours, but His ways are too.

> **For as the heavens are higher than the earth, so are my ways higher than your ways, and my thoughts than your thoughts.**
>
> **Isaiah 55:9**

You may ask yourself, *If God's ways and thoughts are higher than our ways and thoughts, then how can we know them?* Before I tell you how you can know the ways and thoughts of God, you must settle in your heart that His ways and thoughts will always be higher than yours. He is God.

Knowing that fact, however, is no reason you shouldn't get to know God's ways or His thoughts. It just helps you realize that you will always have something new to learn as you grow in the things of God.

Learning about God and His Word is a growing process every day. You will never reach a point of perfection, but you can become more like Him in every area of your life. You should have a deep desire to know God's ways and to think like Him. And when you blow it (which you will do, just like me), ask for forgiveness and ask the Holy Spirit to help you in that area the next time.

God's mercy is new every morning — not just *some* mornings, but *every* morning. Each new day brings a new set of mercies, because His compassions fail not. People's compassion may fail, but God's compassion fails not. You can depend on His compassion, because He is faithful and His faithfulness is great! (Lamentations 3:22,23.) It is so important that you know this, because some days, your ways and thoughts are not like God at all. That is when you need His mercy.

Let's get back to the question, "How can we know God's ways and thoughts even though they are higher than our own?" One way is through the Word of God.

It's so important for you to ask the Holy Spirit to reveal or make known God's Word to you so that when you read the Bible, the words come alive *to* you and *in* you. Once the Word is revealed to you, you will gain knowledge of God and of the abundant life He has planned for you.

It is easier to guard your heart when you know God's Word. And once you know His Word and act upon it, you will reap the benefits of that obedience.

Another way to know the ways and thoughts of God is by the Spirit of God revealing something to you. And it is important to understand that whatever the Holy Spirit reveals can *always* be backed up by God's Word.

...Eye has not seen, nor ear heard, nor have

entered into the heart of man the things which God has prepared for those who love Him.

But God has revealed them to us through His Spirit. For the Spirit searches all things, yes, the deep things of God.

1 Corinthians 2:10, NKJV

The Holy Spirit will reveal the deep things of God — not just surface truths, but the *deep* things of God.

What if someone told you that they were giving you some land that had oil on it? The oil would not really be *on* the land, but *in* it. And if you were going to draw that oil out, you would have to dig deep first to find it and then to get it out of the ground. That is why oil companies have oil rigs.

If you were given land that had oil on it, I know as well as you do that you would do your best to obtain the right machinery to get that oil out. Well, I submit to you that God's Word is much more valuable than oil.

You have to spend time in prayer and in reading the Bible, believing what God said, and then acting upon what He said (that is what faith is). Prayer will break the ground, and faith will dig into it. You must have faith to keep digging when you don't see results right away.

That is what happened to the children of Israel when they waited in the wilderness for Moses to come down from the mountain. They felt that Moses was taking too long, so they allowed themselves to grow weary.

The people went to Aaron and asked him to make them gods to go before them. (Exodus 32:1.) Because they had no patience, they were willing to turn their backs on the true God in order to worship false gods.

The Israelites' real problem was that they had no faith. When things went well, they praised God. When things weren't going according to their wishes, they complained.

Faith will keep you believing God. It will keep you digging in the Word, knowing that God told you to dig there until something is revealed.

It is important to spend quality time with God, a time when you can be alone with Him. Don't allow distractions to steal your time from Him. You must discipline yourself in order to receive the deep things of God. You must discipline yourself to pray. The more truth and revelation you allow God to put into your heart during prayer, the stronger your heart will become.

As you communicate with God and He in turn communicates with you, your heart will be filled with His words and thoughts. When your heart is filled with His words and His thoughts, there is no room left for doubt. Doubt may try to come, but there just won't be any room for it, because the space in your heart will be filled with the Word of God.

I believe your heart can be open to get attacked in different areas. It may get hit by doubt, confusion, jealousy, envy, depression, thoughts of revenge, impatience, lust or greed. But you must be diligent to guard your heart from these and many other harmful things by faith in God's Word.

Before we move on, let me show you in the Word exactly what God thinks about you.

For I know the thoughts that I think toward you, says the Lord, thoughts of peace and not of evil, to give you a future and a hope.

Jeremiah 29:11, NKJV

You should add these words, which are God's thoughts, to your heart. Then if an attack comes, you can use the Word in your heart to fight off the attack. The Word is your weapon, and faith in the Word brings results. If you put good things (the Word) in your heart, then good things will come out of your heart. However, if you allow negative things into your heart, then only negative things will come out of your heart. *You* determine the issues of life that come forth from you.

A good man out of the good treasure of the heart bringeth forth good things: and an evil man out of the evil treasure bringeth forth evil things.

Matthew 12:35

If you don't like the results of what you have allowed to lodge in your heart, you can make a change right now. Don't delay and allow another second to slip by.

Chapter 2

A Heart Not Inflamed

Perhaps now you understand how important it is to know the ways and thoughts of God through His Word. Now you realize that you must fill up your heart with the Word of God, because out of the heart come the issues of life — the results of that which is in you. Do you see how valuable your heart really is?

Your heart becomes even more valuable when it holds "good treasure" — God's Word. The Word of God makes you valuable. Did you know that you are precious? God said that you are a chosen generation, a royal priesthood and a holy nation. (1 Peter 2:9.) Did you know that even your prayers are like a fragrance to God?

> **...and golden vials full of odours, which are the prayers of saints.**
>
> **Revelation 5:8**

I do believe that God is fighting for you, and He wants the best for you. Not only does He care for you, but He has provided you with such blessings as a family, a job, friends and a church home. If you don't have these blessings yet, God has them waiting and available for you. And if you should ever lose any of these blessings, He will restore them to you.

God wants you to enjoy this life. He will give you all things richly to enjoy. (1 Timothy 6:17.) All this good news you must guard in your heart.

You cannot allow the Word to depart from your eyes. (Proverbs 4:21.); you must hide the Word in your heart. (Psalm 119:11.) You guard your heart by guarding the Word in your heart. Satan is only after the Word that is in your heart. While God is thinking good about you, Satan is accusing you. If the enemy can steal God's Word out of your heart, you lose the good results that the Word can produce.

Read Mark 4:14-20. Reading these verses, you can quickly identify that Satan is after the Word and that he will come immediately to steal it. He is only after the Word that is in the *heart*, not in the *head*, of a person. The Word of God will affect your life only when it gets down in your heart — from the head to the heart.

Let me put it this way: When the Word is in your head, you just think about the fact that it may or may not be true to you. But when you allow the Word to get from your head down into your heart, you come to know the value of its truth. Now it is in a place where you must keep it and guard it.

You may be tempted to stop believing the Word, because the results of the Word you are believing may not manifest as soon as you would like. But don't give up. You must be determined to believe what God said, no matter how long it takes — *that* is *faith*.

Satan is after only the Word that is sown in your heart. In Ephesians 6:16, it says that he will throw fiery darts at you. The enemy will throw fiery darts at you to discourage you long enough to stop you.

The word *fiery* in the Greek means to be inflamed with anger, grief and lust. Satan's desire is to hit your heart right in the bull's eye with one of his fiery darts. If Satan can get your heart inflamed with anger, hate, or bitterness — anything that will cause you to give up on the Word of God — he has succeeded in stealing your faith.

36

When you use your faith (Ephesians 6:16 uses the term "the shield of faith"), you are actually activating the Word of God. You can only enjoy victory by exercising faith in God's Word — faith in what God has already said. By proclaiming the truth of God's Word, you are activating the shield of faith.

Let's look at some of the fiery darts that Satan will throw your way and the shield of faith that you must put up against each of these darts:

Fiery Dart No. 1: Being offended.

We must guard our hearts against words that would cause us to get offended. We cannot afford to take offense. When we allow ourselves to get offended, we get hurt.

Hurt, if not dealt with, will cause bitterness, and the Bible says that a root of bitterness will trouble you. (Hebrews 12:15.) Notice that a root of bitterness will trouble not the person you are bitter against, but *you*. And if you are troubled, you will trouble people around you.

Allowing yourself to get offended can turn out to be very devastating for you and for all who come in contact with you on a daily basis. You must learn to forgive and move on, and only the Spirit of God can help you.

Shield of Faith:

And whenever you stand praying, if you have anything against anyone, forgive him, that your Father in heaven may also forgive you your trespasses (Mark 11:25, NKJV).

Fiery Dart No. 2: Cares of the world.

We are *in* the world, but we are not *of* it. All that is in the world are the lust of the eyes, the lust of the flesh, and the pride of life. Cares can only weigh you down and cause you to be ineffective. You are to have a productive life, fulfilling every potential that God has put in you. But you must cast your cares or worries onto the Lord. Only He can handle your problems — you can't.

Shield of Faith:
Casting all your care upon Him; for He careth for you (1 Peter 5:7).

Fiery Dart No. 3: Deceitfulness of riches.

For the love of money is the root of all evil: which while some coveted after, they have erred from the faith, and pierced themselves through with many sorrows.

1 Timothy 6:10

Money is not evil, but the *love of money* is evil. In fact, it is the root of all kinds of evil. Too many people will do deceitful things to get money, position, and power. In Proverbs 15:27, the Bible calls it being "greedy for gain" — greedy for money and greedy for power (the higher the position in life, the more power you have).

But the love of money and being greedy for gain will only lead us to sorrow and trouble. God does want us to prosper in all areas of life, including our finances, but we must do it His way. Proverbs 10:22 says, **The blessing of the Lord, it maketh rich, and he addeth no sorrow with it.**

Shield of Faith:
This book of the law shall not depart out of thy mouth; but thou shalt meditate therein day

and night, that thou mayest observe to do
according to all that is written therein: for then
thou shalt make thy way prosperous, and then
thou shalt have good success (Joshua 1:8).

Fiery Dart No. 4: Doubt.

Doubt is a robber of faith. You can't go forward in
life if you allow doubt to lead you. Either you will be led
by faith or led by doubt. You may say, "I have faith," but
I would ask you, where is your faith? Is it in a person, in
your bank account, in your status in life, in your family
inheritance, in your retirement plan or investment plan,
or in your college degree(s)? There is nothing wrong
with having any of these things, but faith in these natural
things cannot stand up to Satan's fiery darts.

Your faith must be able to stand, and the only
way it will stand is if it is on a solid foundation that can
never be moved. The only foundation that is sure is
God's Word. In Psalm 119:89, it says that God's Word is
settled in heaven, which means it stands firm.

Satan will not try to aim the dart of doubt at your
heart first; he will aim at your head. If he can get doubt
to operate in your thoughts, and if you don't cast down
the negative imaginations that come with those
thoughts, doubt will soon find its way down to your
heart. Doubt has caused many people to give up in life.
You must read God's Word for knowledge, hear God's
Word for faith, and use God's Word for victory.

Shield of Faith:
Casting down imaginations, and every high
thing that exalteth itself against the knowledge
of God, and bringing into captivity every
thought to the obedience of Christ (2 Corinthians

10:5).

You must guard your heart against these four fiery darts of the enemy.

We can quench all of the devil's fiery darts by putting on, keeping on, and using the whole armor of God: the belt of truth, the breastplate of righteousness, the gospel of peace, the shield of faith, the helmet of salvation, and the sword of the Spirit. (Ephesians 6:13-18.)

Although most people like to stop reading about the armor of God at verse 17, I like to continue on to verse 18. This verse is not usually included as a part of the believer's spiritual armor. But to know how to use the armor of God and to keep it on, you must "pray always with all prayer and supplication in the Spirit being watchful (enduring) to the end, with all perseverance and supplication for the saints."

Praying in the Holy Spirit will build you up. (Jude 20.) You will have the courage to fight the good fight of faith. You will realize that victory comes not by your own ability, but only by the ability that God gives you. When those darts start coming toward your head (in other words, your soul or your mind, will and emotions), you must cast down those thoughts of defeat. If you don't, those thoughts will eventually find their way into your heart.

Stay prepared by God's Spirit by praying in the Spirit. Keep the armor of God on by studying the Word of God, going to church where the Word is taught, fellowshiping with others who are stronger in their spiritual walk than you, and walking by faith and not by sight. When you do these things, the future only holds *victory*.

Chapter 3

Receiving From God

The Spirit of the Lord is upon me, because he hath anointed me to preach the gospel to the poor; he hath sent me to heal the brokenhearted, to preach deliverance to the captives, and recovering of sight to the blind, to set at liberty them that are bruised.

Luke 4:18

You may be saying to yourself, *Kathy, I have already allowed my heart to be broken. I didn't know that my heart was valuable; I didn't know it was the place where the Word of God should be hidden. And now my heart, instead of being filled with good treasures, is filled with pollution from the world.*

I must admit, God's Word can't get into my heart, because I have allowed negative words to come in: words of defeat, words of doubt, words of unbelief. Now the only thing that I have to show for what I have allowed in my heart is another bad relationship, a broken home, depression, and confusion. I just don't know how all this will end.

You may be saying this to yourself, but I believe that God has all the answers to your questions. His Word is already settled in heaven, which means the Word stands firm. (Psalm 119:89.) Jesus already paid the price for a broken heart.

By His anointing, Jesus has already healed your

41

broken heart. All you must do now is receive your healing. Go to the Great Physician, Dr. Jesus (the Anointed One), and He will heal (make whole) your heart.

You may feel like you can trust your friends, your spouse, your boss, your pastor, or another man or woman of God with your broken heart. Well, there is nothing wrong with having people you trust enough to share your heart with. But why not go to the Creator who created mankind? He knows all about you, and He knows what no other person knows. He sees into your innermost being, and only He can make your heart whole.

Sometimes we want to wait for hands to be laid on us or for a word to be spoken over us to receive our healing, and this type of ministry is good if God is leading you in that direction. But I'm telling you, I believe right now, right this very minute, God's anointing is in the room with you to heal your heart and to set you free. You need deliverance now, not tomorrow.

The Holy Spirit is here now, right where you are, to free you. God says in His Word, **For I am with you to deliver you, says the Lord** (Jeremiah 1:8).

We can make receiving from God hard. But it is not hard, because He freely gives to us.

Why would He try to make it hard for you to be healed from a broken heart? What would He gain from you struggling and begging to get healed? Not one thing. You may say to yourself, *But it took years for me to get this way.* I know, but it has been more than two thousand years that your deliverance and your healing have been waiting for you. So your deliverance is older than you *and* your problems!

Don't allow your own fears and lack of faith to get in the way of your receiving. If you need healing from a broken heart, stop right now and thank God in Jesus' name for your healing. Then let Him know that you receive your healing, right now. Welcome the Holy Spirit, and allow Him to minister to you, giving Him glory for your healing.

Don't move on to another chapter until you have taken the time to do this. If you don't need God to heal your heart, then allow God to set you free from negative habits. God is here right now to meet your needs. Put your trust fully in Him.

Chapter 4

Ways To Guard Your Heart

There are several ways to guard your heart. I will give you what I believe are the four most important areas in guarding your heart.

Guard Your Heart #1: Guard what you hear.

If any man have ears to hear, let him hear.

And he said unto them, TAKE HEED WHAT YE HEAR: with what measure ye mete, it shall be measured to you: and unto you that hear shall more be given.

Mark 4:23,24

God designed our ears to hear. Have you ever noticed that God created us with one mouth and two ears? Do you think He was trying to tell us something? I do. I think He was trying to tell us that we need to listen more than we need to talk. I believe that every ability God gives to us, we have so that He can receive glory.

The Bible says that faith comes by hearing, and hearing by the Word of God. But doubt (or unbelief) comes by hearing too. However, it doesn't come by the Word of God; doubt comes by hearing words that are *opposite* to God's Word.

That is why you must guard your ears at all times. It must become automatic without even thinking about it. When you hear something contrary to what is in the Bible, you must learn to reject it quickly. If you keep hearing something negative over and over again, it can start to affect your heart. You can even start to believe negative things that you tell yourself, such as what you hear yourself say about you.

For example, I used to sing a song when I was a young child that went something like this: "Everybody hates me, nobody likes me, I'm gonna eat some worms. Fat ones, skinny ones..." I would sing this song out loud to myself. I must admit, it is a dumb song, and I don't know where I learned it. But as a child, I had such a poor self-image of myself, I believed the words to this song. I heard myself sing this song over and over again until I believed its negative report.

Do you know why it is important to go to a church that is teaching the Word of God? Because in that kind of church, you can hear a good report; you will receive the spiritual diet you need. You will hear words that bring life and faith to you.

The Bible says that God's words are spirit and life to you and that faith comes by hearing the Word. (Romans 10:17.) So every time you go to church, you will receive more life and more faith, as long as the Word is being taught by the Spirit of God through an anointed man or woman.

Sometimes people, even Christians, don't want someone to tell them what to do. That can be true even if it is God trying to get their attention through a person's words.

For instance, I remember one time when a fellow Christian got very angry at me because in my message, I mentioned the negative effect that watching soap operas on television will have on a person. In fact, for some reason, every time I got up to deliver a message in that church, I would get on this subject.

Well, I didn't know that this particular person in the congregation had a real problem with watching soap operas. But God knew, and I believe He wanted to set this person free from this habit. Eventually this person stopped coming to the meetings.

At one time in my life, I had experienced almost the same thing. I became hooked on daytime soap operas because I wasn't guarding my ears. I was allowing garbage — lying words, strife-filled words, envious words, adulterous words, hateful words, and depressing words — to enter my ears.

Even though what you hear is a Hollywood script, you get so caught up in those words that your own conversation becomes filled with them. When you surround yourself with negative or positive words, you fill your heart with the abundance of those words, and soon the words will come out of your mouth and shape your lifestyle.

The Bible says to take heed to what you hear. (Mark 4:23.) You are responsible for what you allow yourself to hear on a daily basis. When it says to take heed, it means to be careful about what you are hearing. You must stay alert in this area.

You may have some friends that you need to stop fellowshiping with (my husband breaks this word down as "fellows-in-the-same-ship"), just because of the words they are always saying. For example, if some of your friends enjoy gossiping, and they continue to do so around you after you have asked them to stop, then the next thing you should do is to stop being "in the same ship."

God won't make that decision for you, and the devil wants you to hear wrong things. So *you* must decide what you will allow yourself to hear on a regular basis. You can't shut everybody up around you, but you can choose where you go and who you spend a lot of your time with .You can also decide what you watch on television or listen to on the radio.

When you put value on your ears, you put value on your heart. The old adage, "garbage in and garbage out" is true: If negative words and unbelief are allowed into your heart through what you hear, then negative words and an "I-can't-do-it" attitude will come out.

For instance, if you hear that healing is not for today, then the words "healing is not for today" will come from your heart out of your mouth. Words go in your ears, into your mind, and down to your heart (unless you reject the thoughts).

You can't live on this earth every day wearing earplugs all the time. I know you must go to work (some of you may ride a bus to work), go to the grocery store, and so forth, where it is impossible to avoid all negative words. Or you may turn on the evening news for a few minutes to find out what is going on in the world and immediately hear fearful words.

During the holiday season, sometimes you visit friends and family members who just haven't learned these biblical principles about guarding your heart that you are learning. It would be rude to keep a set of earplugs handy and pop them in whenever someone starts talking negatively. You may want to, but mercy and compassion takes over.

What do you do then? You must fill up your heart with God's Word. Set this as your first priority. Then when you hear words spoken that are against the will of God, you may hear those words with your physical ears, but your mind will reject the words, protecting your heart from the evil report.

Your heart will reject an evil report. If your heart

is full of the Word of God, then your heart can't be full of negative words. You are responsible for what you consume with your ears.

Guard Your Heart #2: Guard your thoughts.

Many, O Lord my God, are they wonderful works which thou has done, and thy thoughts which are to usward; they cannot be reckoned up in order unto thee: if I would declare and speak of them, they are more than can be numbered.

Psalm 40:5

This psalm is a Psalm of David. David knew his God and the magnitude of God's thoughts. You must do as David did: Praise God for His thoughts toward you, because God's thoughts are good and not evil toward you.

God thinks differently than man. God thinks better about you than what you have perhaps been told or what you have told yourself. You must think about yourself the way God thinks about you, for He is sure of the way He thinks. He will never change, and He cannot lie. Here is just one of the thoughts that He thinks about you:

For I know the thoughts that I think toward you, saith the Lord, thoughts of peace, and not of evil, to give you an expected end.

Jeremiah 29:11

So many Christians are defeated because they still think about themselves the way they were when they were in spiritual darkness. Or they may still believe the lie that Satan submitted to them long ago through another person. They may have heard over and over again that they were no good, dumb, or ugly; they may have heard that they would never amount to anything and that nobody wanted them.

If you are in that situation, you must realize that such words were spoken by people who weren't obeying or hearing from God. People who spoke such words just didn't know Him. Now the words that someone else said about you are adversely affecting your life and those who are around you.

The wrong way that you think about yourself not only hurts you, but it will hurt your marriage, your children, your career, your relationship with society, your relationships at church, and your relationship with God. You will think that God thinks about you the same negative way someone else might think about you or the way you think about yourself.

But that is not true. You may think that you are a failure, but God doesn't think that way. His thoughts are of peace, and not evil. He desires to give you an expected end, which means a future and hope. There is no sure future outside of the kingdom of God, and there is no true hope.

When you put your trust in God and obey Him, the success of your future is guaranteed, and hope will become an anchor for your soul, according to Hebrews 6:19. Just think about it: Hope becomes your anchor, secure and firm. It makes you think of a ship on the sea when the anchor is down. The current of the water may get boisterous, but that ship is not going anywhere because the anchor holds it fast. The anchor is smaller than the ship, but its strength keeps the ship secure.

In the same way, hope will actually overpower a hopeless situation. God really does love you, and He finds delight in seeing you prosper in all areas of life.

Now thanks be unto God, which always causeth us to triumph in Christ....

2 Corinthians 2:14

In Christ, you can *always* triumph — not just sometimes, but all the time. Nothing can separate you from God's love, and His good thoughts of you are more than you can number.

Guard Your Heart #3: Guard your mouth.

I will bless the Lord at all times: his praise shall continually be in my mouth. My soul shall make her boast in the Lord: the humble shall hear thereof, and be glad.

Psalm 34:1,2

This is actually a confession that you must decide to make at all times: "I will bless the Lord at all times. His praise shall continually be in my mouth. My soul shall make her boast in the Lord. The humble shall hear thereof and be glad!"

You must decide ahead of time that you will continually bless the Lord. It is an act of your will. Do you know that you can *make* praise come out of your mouth? You alone are totally in charge of your mouth and what comes out of it. That is why it is important to fill your heart with so much of God's Word that it is only natural for the Word to come out of your mouth, especially in the midst of a trial.

One thing I have come to realize is that whatever comes from my mouth that is doubt instead of faith is my fault. I must continually feed on the Word of God so that the Word can continually come forth from me at all times.

How can you praise the Lord at *all* times — not just when things are going smoothly, but when circumstances threaten to shipwreck your faith? This is how: You just *make* yourself boast in the Lord. You make yourself speak faith. You make yourself praise God. You make yourself speak the Word and not the circumstances. (I didn't say it would be easy, but it *is* possible.)

At one time or another, we have all gotten discouraged and started talking about the circumstances. At one time or another, we have all spoken about what we saw — in other words, we walked by sight and not by faith.

But you don't pack up your bags and give up when you mess up; you must stand and keep on standing. Ask for forgiveness and start over again, asking the Holy Spirit for help.

The Holy Spirit dwells within us to help us praise God continually. We cannot do anything on our own. We need God's Spirit guiding us every day.

You guard your heart by guarding your mouth. If you don't guard your mouth, but instead allow yourself to speak any way that you want to speak, then you are headed for disappointment. Your heart may be telling you to believe God, but your mouth speaks out fear. You hear yourself speak negatively, and you start to believe what you hear yourself say.

It is possible for your mouth to speak what is not in your heart. Jesus talked about this when the scribes and the Pharisees questioned Him after Jesus called them hypocrites. In Matthew 15:7,8, Jesus said:

...well did Esaias prophesy of you, saying,

This people draweth nigh unto me with their mouth, and honoureth me with their lips; but their heart is far from me.

Your mouth can speak what is not in your heart. But if you keep speaking negatively, those negative words will eventually get into your heart. Faith comes by hearing the Word of God, and doubt comes by hearing what is opposite to the Word of God.

Your mouth should line up with your heart. The more you put God's Word in your heart, the more your heart will be established in the things of God. Then when a testing comes, your heart will tell you to just stand, be courageous, and be strong.

Your soul (mind, will, emotions) may try to rule you, but your heart (your spirit) will be strong in the Word of God. And with the help of the Holy Spirit, you won't allow what you see or feel to come forth out of your mouth. Instead, you will speak only the Word of God that has been built into your heart in abundance.

Perhaps you are a young Christian, or you may have just received the revelation of the truth that it is the knowledge of and faith in God's Word that will cause you to not be destroyed. It is important to realize that if you don't fill your heart with God's Word, over a period of time your heart will get weaker and weaker. You will actually nullify the few good things that have entered into your heart. You won't have the Word in abundance in your heart.

Your spirit must rule over your flesh and your soul. In James 3, starting at verse 5 (you should read the whole chapter during your study time), it reads:

Even so the tongue is a little member, and boasteth great things. Behold, how great a matter a little fire kindleth!

And the tongue is a fire, a world of iniquity: so is the tongue among our members, that it defileth the whole body, and setteth on fire the course of nature; and it is set on fire of hell.

James 3:5,6

Then in verse 8, it reads: **But the tongue can no man tame; it is an unruly evil, full of deadly poison.**

Let me interject something here. That is why it is so important not to call your children stupid or other negative names. It will poison their minds and eventually their hearts.

The Bible says that no man can tame the tongue; no man has the strength. So do we continue to bless and curse with our mouths? No, it is not saying that, because in verse 10 it reads: **Out of the same mouth proceedeth blessing and cursing. My brethren, these things ought not so to be.**

In other words, speaking wrong words out of our mouths doesn't have to happen. But if we can't tame the tongue, who or what can? We must ask God the same thing that David asked Him in Psalm 141:3, NKJV: **Set a guard, O Lord, over my mouth; Keep watch over the door of my lips.**

This is the only way you can tame your tongue. To get the results you want, you must allow your mouth to work *with* your heart, not *against* it. It will do you no good just to guard your heart and not your mouth, or to guard your mouth and not your heart. They must work together. That is why this third area is so important to you. You guard your heart by guarding your mouth in order to get the victory.

But what saith it? The Word is nigh thee, even in thy mouth, and in thy heart: that is, the word of faith, which we preach....

For with the heart man believeth unto righteousness; and with the mouth confession is made unto salvation.

Romans 10:8,10

You can believe with your heart unto righteousness, but salvation also results from your *confession*. The word *salvation* doesn't only mean eternal life; the Greek word is *soteria*, which means "rescue; safety; deliver; health; salvation; save; and saving."[1] When your confession coming out of your mouth is in line with God's

---

[1]Strong, James. "Greek Dictionary of the New Testament." *In Strong's Exhaustive Condordance of the Bible,* Nashville: Thomas Nelson Publishers, 1990, p. 70.

Word, you will receive health, deliverance, and safety.

Do you see this? Your heart believes, but now your mouth is in agreement with your heart, and confession is made. In other words, your heart is guarded. The seed of the Word that is already sown in your heart will produce good things when your mouth concurs with that seed. What you say will either keep the guard on your heart, or it will let the guard down.

Here are a few more scriptures regarding the mouth:

The mouth of a righteous man is a well of life: but violence covereth the mouth of the wicked.

Proverbs 10:11

The mouth of the just bringeth forth wisdom: but the forward tongue shall be cut out.

Proverbs 10:31

He that keepeth his mouth keepeth his life: but he that openeth wide his lips shall have destruction.

Proverbs 13:3

A man hath joy by the answer of his mouth: and a word spoken in due season, how good is it!

Proverbs 15:23

Guard Your Heart #4: Guard your eyes.

...the commandment of the Lord is pure, enlightening the eyes.

Psalm 19:8

The light of the eyes rejoiceth the heart....

Proverbs 15:30

Your eyes can be full of light or full of darkness.

Your eyes are very important to your heart and to your success in life. You must train your eyes as to what they will look at and what they will not look at.

How often have we allowed our eyes to look at the wrong things? How often have we watched wrong television shows (television is "telling a vision") or movies or looked at ungodly magazines or other ungodly materials?

In Psalm 101:3, it reads: **I will set no wicked thing before mine eyes**.... David said this, but we must choose to say the same thing. And then we must not only say it, but we must do it. We must refuse to set anything wicked before our eyes. Why? Because wicked things (the word *wicked* means "destruction; evil; ungodly; without profit; and worthless") will cause darkness to cloud our eyes and blind our vision, and that will eventually damage our heart.

If "the light of the eyes rejoiceth the heart," then darkness (which is caused by setting your eyes on wicked things) will cause the heart to become evil. When your heart is evil, you won't praise God and walk in faith, trusting in God's Word. Your lifestyle will become unprofitable.

I believe God is not pleased when we are unprofitable in this life. The Bible says, **Herein is my Father glorified, that ye bear much fruit...** (John 15:8)..

Your physical eyes are very important to your spiritual heart. Advertisers understand the importance of eyes. Why do you suppose they put up big billboards on the side of the road?

For example, cigarette and alcohol advertisers try to make smoking and drinking look appealing. They use the right models in the right lighting with the right colors. Their objective is to make those billboards so inviting that if you are not smoking or drinking, you may start wanting to at least want to try it.

Believe me, if billboards didn't work, companies wouldn't use them. People can't drive blindfolded. For many Christians who are rooted in God's Word, billboards won't affect them, but other things can.

For instance, no matter how long you have been a Christian, you cannot watch X-rated movies and not have them affect your heart. If you allow that kind of evil junk to enter in through your eyes, it will mess up your vision in life because it will mess up your heart. Your heart won't be rejoicing; it will be destroyed.

As Christians living in a dark world, we must always have more and more of the Word before our eyes. We must allow the Word to set a standard in our lives.

The entrance of thy words giveth light; it giveth understanding unto the simple.

Psalm 119:130

You must spend quality time in the Bible, studying it and applying it to your life. It will take consistency, discipline, and an abiding love for the Word of God. If there are areas of your life where darkness still resides, allow the entrance of God's Word to come in and bring light. When light comes, understanding and knowledge come.

The Bible says all that is in the world is the lust of the eyes, the lust of the flesh, and the pride of life. (1 John 2:16.) Men, that is why it is not good to take that second or third look at a woman who is not your wife (women can also have this problem with the opposite sex). A look can lead to lust, which can lead you into adultery.

But I say unto you, that whosoever looketh on a woman to lust after her hath committed adultery with her already in his heart.

Matthew 5:28

Sounds like a person using his eyes for the wrong thing is a serious matter, doesn't it? Well, it is, and it is robbing strong men and women of God of their full potential.

Satan will submit various types of bait for your eyes to see. If you take the bait, he has your heart. The bait that may work for you may not work for someone else. Satan knows the right bait to use.

Even the fishing world knows the importance of the right bait. Visit a sporting goods store sometime where they sell fish bait. I did, and I couldn't believe the huge number of types of bait! It is unbelievable. There are different baits for all kinds of different fish. For instance, if you want to catch salmon, you must buy the kind of bait they like. Bait comes in various shapes, colors, length, width, sizes and textures.

As I looked at all the types of fishing bait, I couldn't help but think about the bait Satan uses on people. Satan uses various temptations as bait to hook people.

That is why you are not to yield to temptation. But a temptation to sin can look like something you personally would enjoy. That temptation is bait just for you.

And when the woman saw that the tree was good for food, and that it was pleasant to the eyes...

Genesis 3:6

The problem wasn't that the woman (Eve) saw the tree, but that she never saw that it was *good for food* — something to consume upon her own lust. The source of the problem came when Satan questioned Eve about what God said (Genesis 3:1). When a person questions what God says, he is questioning His Word. So Satan caused Eve to doubt the Word of God, and after that the tree (the bait) looked good for food to her. Can you see what was going on in that situation?

You must allow God's words to stay before your eyes and to enter your heart, because the entrance of His words give light and understanding. As you feed upon God's Word, you will know when Satan is putting out bait for you.

The Bible tells us that we are not to be ignorant of Satan's devices: **Lest Satan should get an advantage of us: for we are not ignorant of his devices** (2 Corinthians 2:11). That word *devices* mean "purpose."[2] Satan's purpose is to steal, kill, and destroy you, but he can't do it if you know the purpose behind his bait and guard your heart against it.

The more your eyes feed on negative movies, books, and so forth, the more you invite darkness to enter in through your eyes and fill your heart. Then you become too weak to pass by any little temptation or bait that Satan puts on a hook. And if you happen to get hooked, you are too weak to escape.

You see, the exit door is always there. As a Christian, you should never be unable to get out of a temptation or off Satan's "hook." Just read Second Corinthians 10:13.

Learn to discipline your eyes by the Word of God, and you will guard your heart.

---

[2]Strong, James. "Greek Dictionary of the New Testament." *In Strong's Exhaustive Condordance of the Bible,* Nashville: Thomas Nelson Publishers, 1990, p. 50.

Conclusion

There are many things we must guard against to guard our hearts. We must guard against pride, hate, worrying, prejudice, strife, envy, a negative past, and a list of many other things. Each day is a new day to guard our hearts against anything that would cause it to become hard against people and especially against God.

The Spirit of God will correct you more and more as you submit yourself to Him. God's compassion and mercies are new every morning. It is because of His faithfulness that He doesn't give up on you.

In Philippians 4:6,7, NKJV, it reads:

Be anxious for nothing, but in everything by prayer and supplication, with thanksgiving, let your requests be made known to God;

and the peace of God, which surpasses all understanding, will guard your hearts and minds through Christ Jesus.

Your daily lifestyle (the choices of what you allow in your heart) will determine how much victory you will enjoy in this life. What you allow into your heart is what will come forth from your life. So if you want abundant life and victory in every situation, make sure that you *guard your heart!*

Steps To Receive Jesus
As Your Personal Savior

You cannot do anything successfully without God's strength and wisdom. But the first step is to receive Him as the Lord and Savior of your life. What good would it be if you gained the whole world, but lost your soul? Say this prayer out loud:

God, I realize I need You in my life. I believe that You sent Your Son, Jesus Christ, to die on the cross for me and that You raised Him from the dead. I am a sinner, and I ask You to forgive me of my sins and to give me eternal life. I confess Jesus as my Lord and the Master of my life; I turn my back on sin. Thank You, Father, for saving me and for giving me eternal life and a new direction in this life. In Jesus' name. Amen.

DATE:_____

SIGNATURE:_____

Additional copies of
Guard Your Heart
are available from your local bookstore,
or from:

Harrison House
P. O. Box 35035
Tulsa, OK 74153

To contact the author, write:

Kathy Lynette Shorter
P.O. Box 44800
Tacoma, WA 98444